Denali National Park

ALASKA

Glacier Bay National Park

Grand Canyon National Park

ARIZONA

Petrified Forest National Park

ARIZONA

Saguaro National Park

ARIZONA

Death Valley National Park

CALIFORNIA AND NEVADA

Joshua Tree National Park

CALIFORNIA

Kings Canyon National Park

CALIFORNIA

Yosemite National Park

CALIFORNIA

Rocky Mountain National Park

COLORADO

Great Sand Dunes National Park

COLORADO

Mesa Verde National Park

COLORADO

Black Canyon of Gunnison National Park

COLORADO

Yellow Stone National Park

IDAHO

Mammoth Cave National Park

KENTUCKY

Glacier National Park

MONTANA

Great Basin National Park

NEVADA

Carlsbad Caverns National Park

NEW MEXICO

White Sands National Park

Theodore Roosevelt National Park

NORTH DAKOTA

Great Smoky Mountains National Park

NORTH CAROLINA

Badlands National Park

SOUTH DAKOTA

Arches National Park

UTAH

Bryce Canyon National Park

UTAH

Capitol Reef National Park

UTAH

Shenandoah National Park

VIRGINIA

Mount Rainier National Park

WASHINGTON

North Cascades National Park

WASHINGTON

Olympic National Park

WASHINGTON

Grand Teton National Park

WYOMING